£1.30

Megan Webster & Libby Castañón

Crosstalk

Communication tasks and games for students of
English at the elementary level

Student's Book 1

Oxford University Press

The authors would like to thank the teachers at the Southern Branch of the
Anglo-Mexican Institute in Mexico City, who so willingly piloted the
material for *Crosstalk* and provided valuable comments for the series.

Illustrations by David Till, Anne Morrow, Carl Keighley

Photographs by Lance Browne

*We are grateful to the following organizations for their help with
photographs:*
Associated Newspapers Group Ltd., Berni Inns, Walton Street, Oxford,
Camera Press, Columbia Pictures Ltd., The Cotswold Lodge Hotel,
Oxford, Daily Telegraph Colour Library, Dyson Perrins Laboratory,
University of Oxford, Mary Evans Picture Library, Keystone Press Agency
Ltd., The Official Elvis Presley Fan Club, Mr. and Mrs. J. R. Parke, Radio
Times Hulton Picture Library, Royal College of Music, Scottish Health
Education Unit, Scottish Widows Fund and Life Assurance Society,
Spanish National Tourist Office.

Contents

Introduction

To the teacher

Book One provides ideas and material for conversation practice at the elementary stage of language learning. Its principal aim is to bridge the gap between the language lesson and real world encounters in the target language through spontaneous use of language in natural or simulated situations. It is meant to be used as a regular supplement to the textbook when the student has learnt the structures needed for a given session. These structures are listed in the Teacher's Book to guide the teacher in his choice at different stages of the syllabus.

The amount of conversation which a student can sustain depends largely on the number of structures he has acquired. Thus a brief period of conversation may be anticipated in the first session, and a gradual lengthening of the conversation span as the student's linguistic resources increase. If conversation practice is instituted early and given regularly in the course, the student will gain an operational command of language at each level of learning which will gradually lead to fluency and accuracy.

The re-use of language items, which is the concern of every conscientious teacher, is implicit in conversation. Moreover, the satisfaction experienced by the student on being able to respond or voice his ideas in the target language, will increase his motivation to learn.

To the student

This book is meant for students who are anxious to speak the language in a natural way while they are learning it. It is designed for adolescent and adult beginners, and is particularly useful for those working towards examinations with an oral component such as the Cambridge First Certificate in English, as it demands constant use of the basic structures and provides practice of a wide range of everyday vocabulary and expressions.

Description of the course

The course comprises three books for the elementary, pre-intermediate, and intermediate levels respectively. There are twenty structured sessions in each book. The sessions have a stimulus to generate open class discussion and a transfer. The latter may take the form of small group discussion, role playing, problem solving or a game.

Each book has an accompanying cassette of dialogues and passages. The purpose of the tapes is twofold: to expose the student to a variety of language and voices, and provide a situation to stimulate conversation.

The Teacher's Book contains clear guidelines in methodology, a list of the essential structures, tapescripts, and examples of the kind of conversation which can be expected in each session. The Teacher's

Book, which covers all three of the students' books in the series, is an integral part of the course and will be particularly helpful for those teachers who know the value of conversation practice, but are apprehensive about 'letting their students go', so to speak, at the early stages of language learning.

Although the sessions are roughly structured to follow a standard basic language syllabus, the teacher need not of course work through the book, but can pick and choose according to the needs and interests of the class. He should also be ready to adapt the ideas in the book to meet the interests of his particular group. There is considerable variation of stimulus and transfer in order to attract and hold the student's attention. In addition, the course seeks to maintain a reasonable level of cultural and educational content.

1 Hello!

A Open class discussion

1 Look at the photographs and listen to the conversation on the tape.

2 What are the people saying?

B Getting to know your classmates

Go around and meet the people in your class. Greet them, say who you are, ask their name, then introduce someone you know to them.

hi!
nice/pleased to
  meet you
this is . . .

2 What is it?

A Class game

Look at the pictures and the words beside them. Then listen to the sounds on the tape and guess what they are.

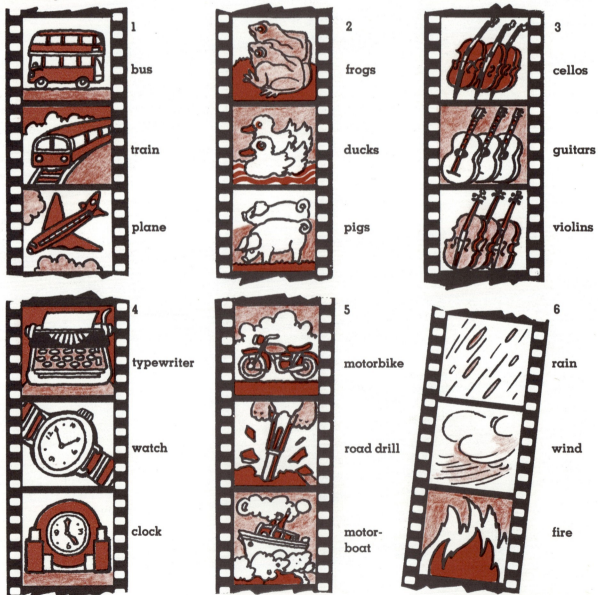

1 bus
   train
   plane

2 frogs
   ducks
   pigs

3 cellos
   guitars
   violins

4 typewriter
   watch
   clock

5 motorbike
   road drill
   motor-
   boat

6 rain
   wind
   fire

B Group game

1 What are these photographs of?
Can you guess? The answers are
in the box. Find them and write
them under the photographs.
Then check your answers with the
rest of the class.

hat	book
toothbrush	cars
shoes	telephone
lemon	bottle
chair	bananas
forks	football

1

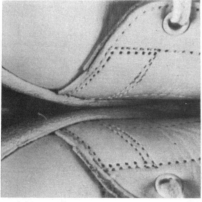

4

5

2

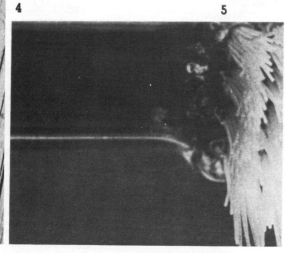

3   **6**

2 Choose a familiar object and
mime it to your group. The group
should guess and ask, 'Is it a . . .'
or 'Is that a . . . ?'

I think
I know
I don't know
Let me see
perhaps
I'm sure

3 You're lucky!

A Open class discussion

1 Here is only half the conversation between the man in the lost property office and Mrs Dexter. What is the other half?

2 Now listen to the tape. Is your dialogue similar?

Hello, is that the lost property office?

_____

Ah. Is my suitcase there?

_____ ?

My name's Nicole Dexter.

_____ ?

It's 6 Green Square, London W.2.

_____ ?

No, it isn't. It's small.

_____ ?

It's blue with a red handle.

_____ ?

No, it's old and the lock's broken.

_____

Oh good! Thank you.

3 Role Playing

Roles: Man in Lost Property Office and person enquiring about a lost article.

1 This is the form for Mrs Dexter's lost suitcase.

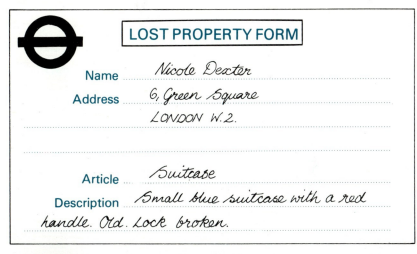

LOST PROPERTY FORM

Name ... *Nicole Dexter*
Address ... *6, Green Square*
LONDON W.2.

Article ... *Suitcase*
Description ... *Small blue suitcase with a red handle. Old. Lock broken.*

Fill in this form for *your* lost property.

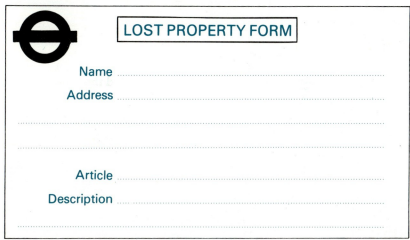

LOST PROPERTY FORM

Name ....
Address ....
....
....
Article ....
Description ....

2 Imagine you are at the Lost Property Office. Act out the conversation with the attendant of the Lost Property Office.

3 Change roles.

heavy	coat
light	satchel
round	Ah . . . Let me see.
rectangular	Well
square	You're lucky.
umbrella	It's here
wallet	I'm sorry
radio	Oh dear!

4 Guess who my 'hero' is

A Open class discussion

1 Look at the picture. Who is the girl's 'hero', and where is he from? Why do you think she likes him? Give your opinion of him.

2 Listen to the tape and say why the girl likes him.

3 What do you think of the people in the photographs?

B Group game

1 Write down the information about *your* hero or heroine (your idol or someone you admire).

Name...
Nationality.....................................
Age ....
Occupation...................................
Description ....

2 Now take it in turns to guess one another's "heroes" by asking questions. For example:

Is he from . . . ?
How old is . . . ?
Is he/she a . . . ? (etc.)

handsome	singer
good-looking	musician
attractive	politician
beautiful	he's so . . .
sexy	I like . . . very
intelligent	much
marvellous	I don't like . . . at
clever	all
actor	that's right
actress	about twenty-five

5 What's the matter?

A Open class discussion

1 Look at the picture on this page.
Where are these people? What are
they doing? Say what they are
wearing and describe them.

2 Listen to the tape, and
complete the following
information about the patient:

Name
Age
What patient can do
What patient can't do
Why can't she?

3 Now talk about the patient, and
say what's the matter with her.

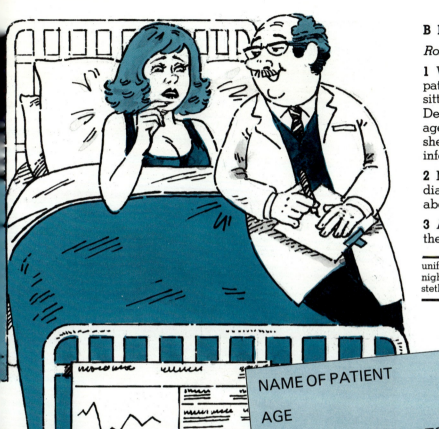

B Role playing

Roles: doctor and patient.

1 Work in pairs. Look at the patient on the right. The doctor is sitting on the patient's arm. Decide on the patient's name and age, what she can move, and what she can't move. Then fill in the information in the space provided.

2 Make up, and act out, a similar dialogue to the one on the tape, about this patient.

3 Act out your dialogue in front of the class.

uniform	middle-aged
nightdress	broken
stethoscope	

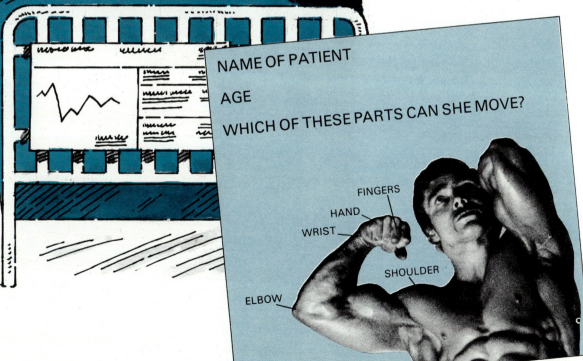

NAME OF PATIENT

AGE

WHICH OF THESE PARTS CAN SHE MOVE?

FINGERS

HAND

WRIST

SHOULDER

ELBOW

6 Eating out

A Open class discussion

1 Fiona and Colin are eating out today. Imagine, and fill in, the missing part of the conversation between them and the waiter.

Waiter Here's the menu.

Fiona Ah, thank you. What's the soup of the day?

Waiter It's celery soup.

Fiona _____?

Waiter It's excellent.

Colin _____?

Waiter Yes, the salmon's fresh today.

Fiona I'd like _____.

Colin I'll have _____.

Waiter Very good, Sir.
Waiter Anything to drink, Sir?

Colin _____.

Waiter Red or white?

Colin _____.

Waiter Very good, Sir.
Colin _____.

Waiter For dessert? Apple pie, chocolate cake or ice-cream.

Fiona I want _____.

Colin _____.

2 Listen to the tape. Is your conversation the same as theirs? What do they order? What kind of wine does Colin ask for?

I like	delicious
I don't like	tasty
I want	tasteless
I'd like	fattening
I'll have	

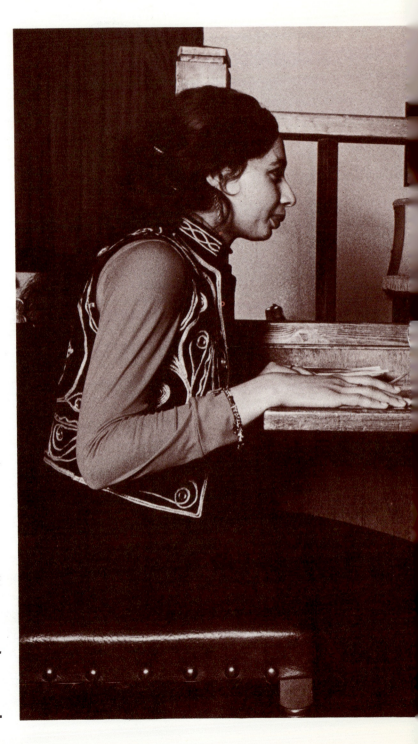

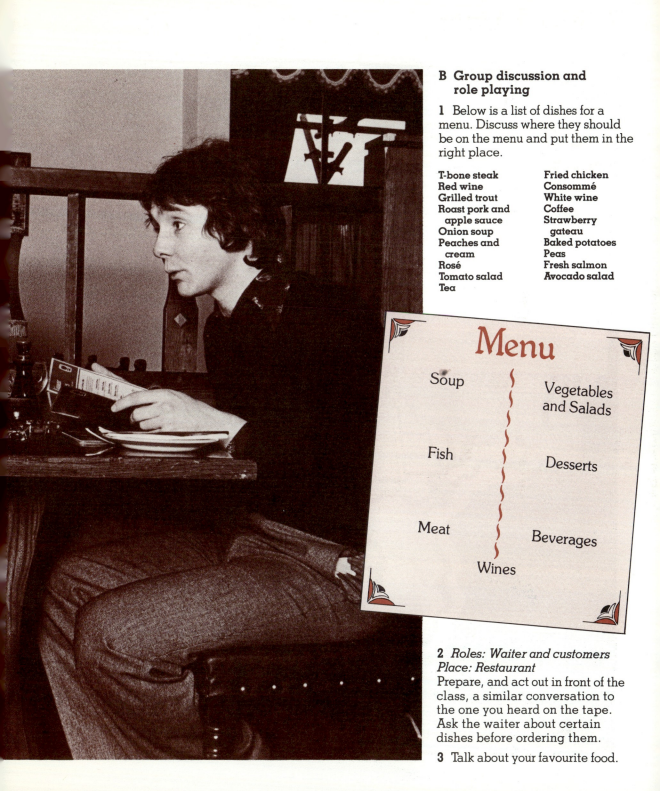

B Group discussion and role playing

1 Below is a list of dishes for a menu. Discuss where they should be on the menu and put them in the right place.

T-bone steak
Red wine
Grilled trout
Roast pork and
 apple sauce
Onion soup
Peaches and
 cream
Rosé
Tomato salad
Tea

Fried chicken
Consommé
White wine
Coffee
Strawberry
 gateau
Baked potatoes
Peas
Fresh salmon
Avocado salad

Menu

Soup

Fish

Meat

Vegetables
and Salads

Desserts

Beverages

Wines

2 *Roles: Waiter and customers*
Place: Restaurant
Prepare, and act out in front of the class, a similar conversation to the one you heard on the tape. Ask the waiter about certain dishes before ordering them.

3 Talk about your favourite food.

7 It's a bargain

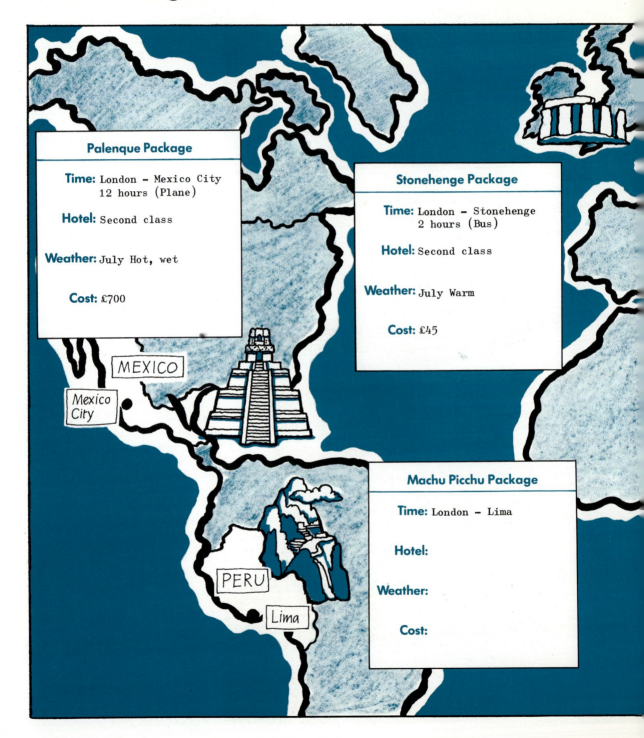

Palenque Package

Time: London – Mexico City
12 hours (Plane)

Hotel: Second class

Weather: July Hot, wet

Cost: £700

Stonehenge Package

Time: London – Stonehenge
2 hours (Bus)

Hotel: Second class

Weather: July Warm

Cost: £45

Machu Picchu Package

Time: London – Lima

Hotel:

Weather:

Cost:

MEXICO

Mexico City

PERU

Lima

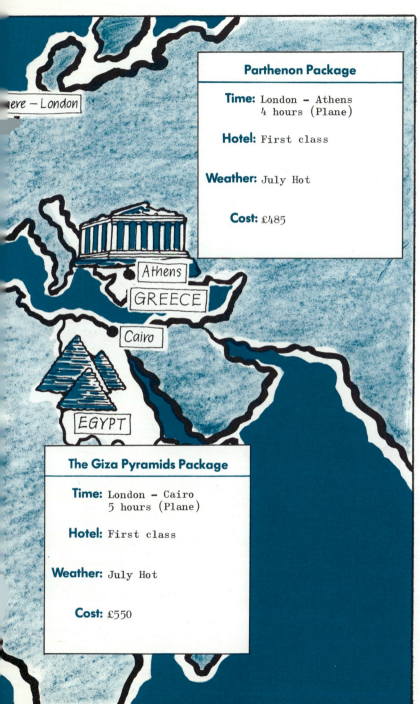

Parthenon Package

Time: London – Athens
4 hours (Plane)

Hotel: First class

Weather: July Hot

Cost: £485

ere – London

Athens

GREECE

Cairo

EGYPT

The Giza Pyramids Package

Time: London – Cairo
5 hours (Plane)

Hotel: First class

Weather: July Hot

Cost: £550

A Open class discussion

1 Look at the map. It gives information about four package holidays. Say exactly where Palenque, Stonehenge, the Parthenon, and the Giza Pyramids are.

2 Listen to the tape, and fill in the information on the Machu Picchu package in the space provided on the map.

3 Listen to the tape again. Say which package the customer chooses, and why.

B Role playing

Roles: travel agent and customer

1 The customer asks the travel agent for information about two of the packages and then chooses one.

2 Change roles.

3 *Roles: friends*
Go around the class and find out about the packages other students have chosen. Ask them where they are going, what the weather's like in July, and how much the package costs.

In north/ south/east/ west . . .	It takes . . .
	How much does it cost?
by bus/plane	That sounds nice
I'm interested in . . .	I see
	What about . . . ?
How long does it take . . . ?	I'd like . . .

8 To let

A Open class discussion

1 Look at the photograph of the block of flats and read the advertisement beside it. Then listen to the tape and say where the flat is, how many rooms it has, what the rent is, etc.

2 Would you like to live in this flat? Why/why not?

B Role playing

1 Look at the photograph of the house and read the advertisement beside it. Decide where the house is, what it's near, what it has, and what the rent is. Write down the description.

Description

_____

_____

_____

_____

_____

_____

2 *Roles: owner of house and house hunter*
Call up and find out about the house.

ACCOMMODATION

BED-SITTING ROOM suitable young professional woman, use of kitchen, Summertown— Tel 788 1501

FLAT TO LET Ideal for young married couple. Reasonable rent. Call 303 6215 between 12 and 2

GIRL wanted to share farmhouse; 6 miles from city

C Group discussion

1 Talk about your house or flat and describe it. Ask your group about theirs.

2 Describe the house or flat you'd like to have.

HOUSE RENTALS

FURNISHED BUNGALOW to let, Southmoor, no students. Tel Woodstock 812328

HOUSE TO LET Big modern house with garden. Ideal for large family. Call 624 5235 after 6 p.m.

COUNTRY COTTAGE short rental, two bedrooms, large garden.

twelve storey building	spacious
central-heating	quiet/noisy
lift (or elevator)	I'd like
fireplace	I wouldn't like
upstairs	What's it like?
downstairs	I'm calling about
suburbs	That sounds
modern	nice/awful

9 Buying a pet

A Open class discussion

1 Below are the names of different pets. Say which ones are in the pet-shop.

  white mice
  canaries
  kittens
  monkeys
  hamsters
  snakes
  puppies
  rabbits
  tropical fish

2 Describe the pets and say where they are in the pet-shop. Which of them do you like?

3 Listen to the tape and say:

  which pet David wants
  which pet Barbara wants
  which one they buy
  what else they buy

B Role playing and discussion

1 *Roles: pet-shop assistant and customers*
Pretend you are in a pet-shop buying a pet

2 Change roles.

3 Describe and talk about the pets you or your friends have. Say what they eat, and where you/they keep them.

cage	sweet
aquarium	fluffy
perch	cuddly
kennel	dangerous
collar	ugly
lead	dirty
pretty	I keep it in . . .
beautiful	I'd like a . . .
friendly	I'll take the . . .

10 Take my advice

A Open class discussion

1 Look at the photograph, and describe the people and what they are doing.

2 Find out if any students in the class smoke, and why and when they smoke. Ask what the smokers think of the advice given below. Then give them your advice.

3 See if you can complete this conversation between a smoker and a non-smoker. Include some of the advice given below.

Smoker (cough, cough)
Non-smoker That's a bad cough.
Smoker Yes (coughs) it's because I smoke.
Non-smoker _____?
Smoker Thirty a day.
Non-smoker _____
Smoker I know it's dangerous for my health.
Non-smoker _____
Smoker It's easy to say. But how?
Non-smoker _____
Smoker That's a good idea.
Non-smoker _____
Smoker But I like a cigarette before breakfast.
Non-smoker Eat an apple instead.
Smoker It's no good (cough, cough) I can't give it up.

4 Now listen to the tape and say if your dialogue is the same.

cigarette holder	go on a diet
filter	put out a cigarette
fattening foods	follow advice
sweets	worry about
salads	That's a good idea
a heavy smoker	It's no good/use
a chain smoker	It's easy to say
instead	Give it up

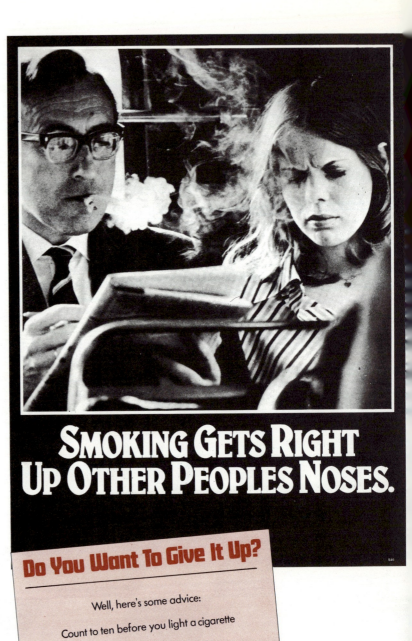

SMOKING GETS RIGHT UP OTHER PEOPLES NOSES.

Do You Want To Give It Up?

Well, here's some advice:

Count to ten before you light a cigarette

Buy only one packet at a time

Don't smoke before breakfast

Don't carry matches or a lighter

B Role playing — in pairs.

Roles: over-weight person and under-weight person.

1 Decide on your role—overweight person or underweight person. Ask your partner to think of advice for you. You should think of advice for your partner. Write down the advice.

2 Take turns at advising each other, and say what you think of the advice given to you.

ADVICE	ADVICE
1 _____	1 _____
2 _____	2 _____
3 _____	3 _____
4 _____	4 _____
5 _____	5 _____

11 Who does what at home?

A Open class discussion

1 Traditional roles in the family are changing. Describe the photograph and say what is unusual about it.

2 Listen to the conversation on the tape. The Webb family are talking. Who do you think does most of the work in the house? Say why nobody helps Mrs Webb with the baby.

3 Say whether this kind of conversation is typical of modern families.

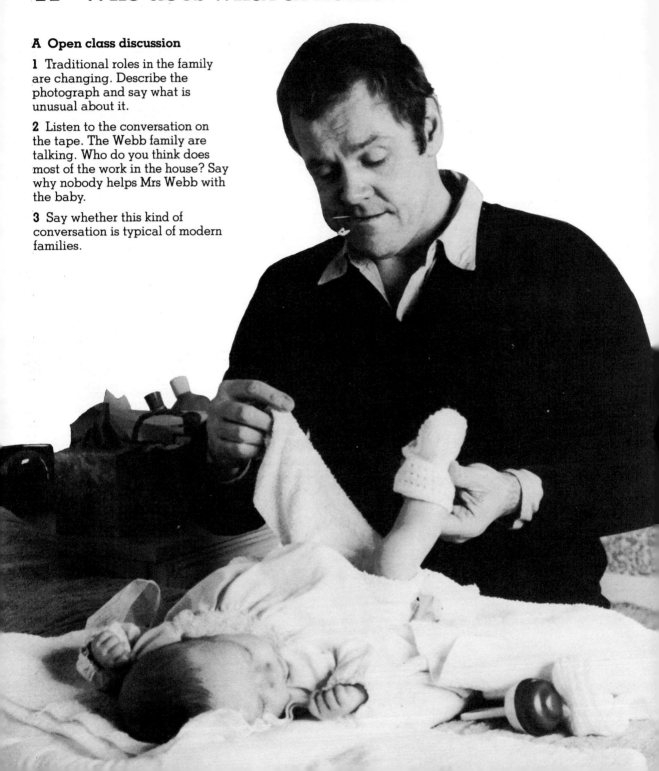

B Group discussion

1 Write down the jobs which the members of your family do in the house. Look at the example given.

MEMBER OF FAMILY	JOB	HOW OFTEN
Sister	Makes the beds	Sometimes

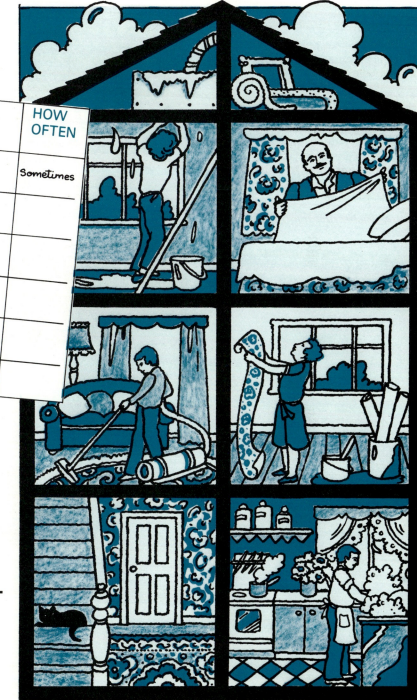

2 Now talk about who does what in your house.

3 Say whether you are all happy with the arrangement.

complain	lay the table
help	make the beds
clean/dust/tidy	lazy
shave	helpful
pick up	tired
safety pin	in a hurry
change a nappy	hardly ever
do the washing up	occasionally
do the shopping	

12 A visit to London

A Open class discussion

1 Study the map, and say what there is to see and do in the West End of London.

2 Listen to the conversation on the tape and say:

what the tourist particularly wants to do
how much time he has
what he can do in that time

B Role playing

Roles: Tourist and Information Clerk

1 You're staying at the Park Hotel, and you have two days to see the West End. Make a list of all the things you want to do.

_____

_____

_____

_____

_____

2 Now ask the Information Clerk to help you work out a suitable programme.

3 Change roles.

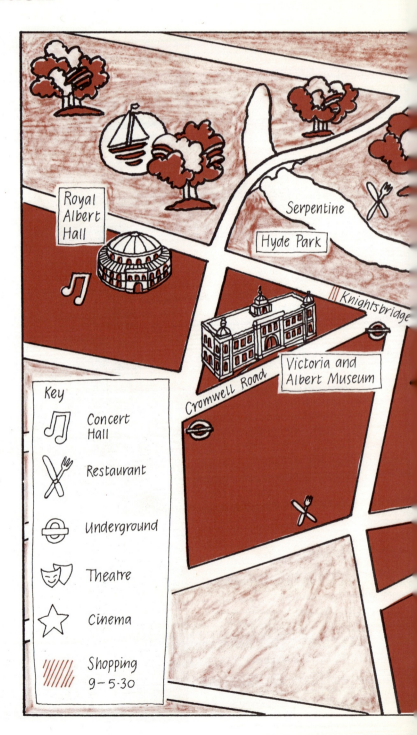

go sightseeing	a lot of/lots of
go shopping	on the first/second
take a taxi/bus/the	day
underground	to start with
have lunch	afterwards
open at	let me see
close at	good/wonderful

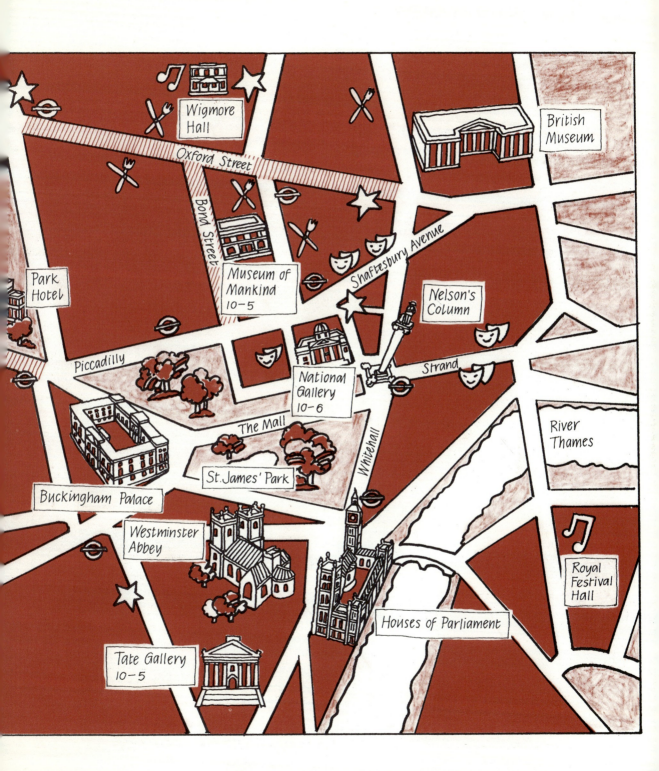

13 The way it was

A Open class discussion

1 Listen to the tape and write down the information asked for below.

Torremolinos
    Number of hotels
    Number of restaurants
    Number of cafeterias
    Number of golf courses
    Number of camping sites
    Number of conference centres
    Pollution

2 Describe Torremolinos as it is today. Say what was different about it 20 years ago.

3 Which do you find attractive; Torremolinos as it was or Torremolinos as it is now? Say why.

A modern beach

A beach twenty years ago

B Group discussion

1 Describe your village, town or city, or a place you know, as it is now, and as it was some years ago. Say what there was then, and what there is now.

2 Talk about places you like for a holiday and say what there is there.

river	smog
lake	traffic jams
mountain	hundreds of
tall building	crowds of
luxury hotel	I like
narrow/wide	I don't like
streets	I can't stand
motorways	It's a pity
noise	

Key to pictures

1 Henry Purcell (1659-95). English. Born and died London. Important 17th cent. composer. Well known songs: "When I am laid in earth", "Nymphs and Shepherds".

2 Gustav Holst (1874-1934). Swiss. Lived part life in England. Played piano and organ. Developed neuralgia in one hand—changed to trombone. "The Planets", "Hymn of Jesus".

3 The Beatles (contemporary). English.

4 Elvis Presley (1935-77). American. Called Father of Rock.

5 Wolfgang Mozart (1756-1791). Austrian. Child prodigy. First concerto at 5. Famous works: "Requiem", "Jupiter Symphony".

6 Benjamin Britten (1913-76). English. Child prodigy. Composed chamber and choral music at 9. "Peter Grimes", "Billy Budd", operas.

7 Ludwig von Beethoven (1770-1827). German. Composed hundreds of works, even when deaf.

8 Luciano Berio (1925-). Italian. Electronic music. Composed "Thema (Omaggio a Joyce)" in 1958.

A Open class discussion

1 Choose a picture of a composer you'd like to know more about. Ask someone in the class who the person is, when and where he was born, when he died (if he isn't alive now), and what he composed, etc.

2 Are you familiar with any pieces of music written by these composers? Mention some that you like, or dislike, and say why you feel this way about them.

B Group discussion

1 Talk about your favourite music, and say where you usually hear it. Do you have any records? Tell your group about them.

2 Do you or any members of your family play a musical instrument? If so, say which ones and how well.

born in	classical
died in	folk
a record of	modern
listen to	electronic
can't stand	in the evening
play records	once in a while
still alive	once a week/
it doesn't say	month/year
soft/loud/harsh	occasionally
magnificent	not very often
awful	hardly ever
melodious	

15 Getting to work

Hundreds of working hours are lost every day because of transport problems.

A Open class discussion

1 Describe the scenes in the two photographs.

2 A woman is doing a survey on transport in cities. She's using the questionnaire below to get information.
Listen to the tape of one of her interviews and write down the answers she receives.

QUESTIONNAIRE

1 How do you usually get to work?

2 How far is your work from your home?

3 How long does it usually take you?

4 What time do you leave home?

5 Did you arrive on time today?

6 Do you think transport is a problem in this city?

3 Tell the class about this man's journey to work, and what he says about transport in his city.

by bus/train/ underground etc.	traffic jam
get on a bus/train	lorry
walk to school/ work	platform
be on time	excuse me
to arrive late	of course
one of them, two of them, all of them	you're welcome

4 Class survey: Now write a similar questionnaire to find out how your classmates come to school, how long it takes them, etc.

Questionnaire	1	2
1		
2		
3		
4		
5		
6		

5 Interview two people in the class, and write their answers in the spaces provided.

B Group discussion

Talk about the results of your questionnaire:

How many people did your group interview?
How many of them come to school by bus? etc.
How many of them arrived late today?
How many say there is a transport problem?

Decide whether there is a serious transport problem in your town or city.

16 Strange encounters

A Open class discussion

1 Describe what you see in these photographs. Do you know *exactly* what the first photograph is of?

2 Listen to the conversation on the tape between three students, Peter, Byron, and Mary Lou and say what they're talking about. What is Peter's story? What experience did he have in Scotland? Do the others believe him? Which of them believe in UFOS?

3 Say whether *you* believe in UFOS and the Loch Ness Monster. What have you heard, or read, about such things?

1

2

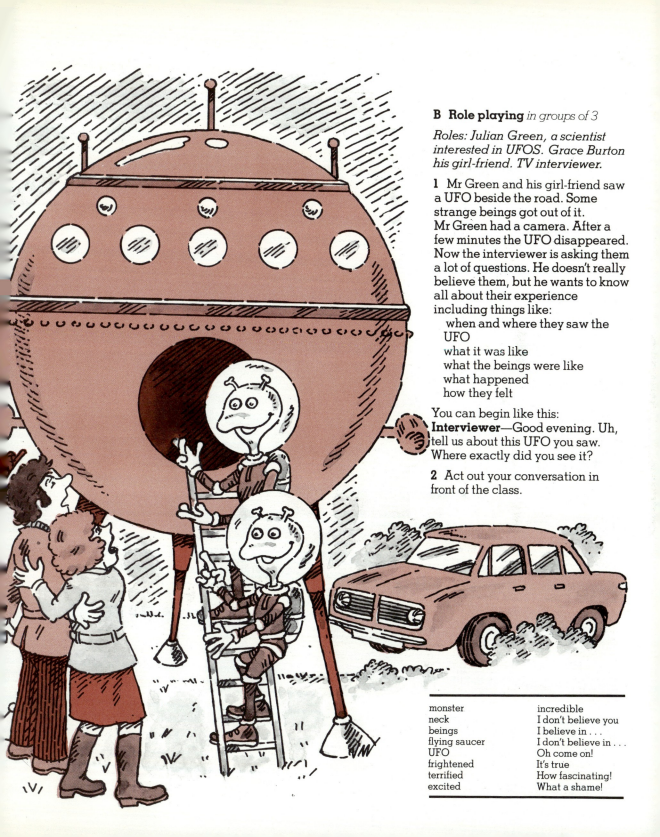

B Role playing *in groups of 3*

Roles: Julian Green, a scientist interested in UFOS. Grace Burton his girl-friend. TV interviewer.

1 Mr Green and his girl-friend saw a UFO beside the road. Some strange beings got out of it. Mr Green had a camera. After a few minutes the UFO disappeared. Now the interviewer is asking them a lot of questions. He doesn't really believe them, but he wants to know all about their experience including things like:

when and where they saw the UFO
what it was like
what the beings were like
what happened
how they felt

You can begin like this:
Interviewer—Good evening. Uh, tell us about this UFO you saw. Where exactly did you see it?

2 Act out your conversation in front of the class.

monster	incredible
neck	I don't believe you
beings	I believe in . . .
flying saucer	I don't believe in . . .
UFO	Oh come on!
frightened	It's true
terrified	How fascinating!
excited	What a shame!

17 Getting married

A Open class discussion

1 Describe the scene in the two wedding photographs.

2 Read the text on Catherine and Simon's wedding. Then listen to the tape and fill in the information about Cilla and John's wedding.

3 Discuss the differences between the two weddings. Mention clothes, reception, and cost etc.

Catherine and Simon

Catherine Miller's white wedding cost £950. Her mother, Mrs Hilary Miller, paid for the £90 wedding dress and for the two week honeymoon in the Bahamas. Catherine paid £63 for the material to make the bridesmaids' dresses and £45 for bouquets. The bridegroom wore a hired grey morning suit. The reception for a hundred guests at the Imperial Hotel cost £650, and the party continued in the evening at the Millers' home.

Cilla and John

Type of wedding ....
Cost ....
Reception ....
Clothes: Cilla ....
          John ....
Honeymoon ....

B Group discussion

1 Talk about a wedding you have
been to, or the wedding you
would like to have.

or Say when and where you met
your husband/wife, and when you
got engaged and married.
Describe your wedding.

2 How important is a wedding?
Say whether you think marriage is
old fashioned.

veil	on the 6th of
top hat	August
lace	get married to
smart	spend on
simple	Well um . . .
elegant	It looks like . . .
in 1963	That sounds . . .
in July	How nice!
meet in/at	It cost the earth.

18 A stranger in town

A Open class discussion

1 Describe the scenes in the photographs and say what the people are doing. Also try to guess what they're saying.

2 On the tape are the two conversations.
a Listen to the first one and tell the class which street the stranger is looking for, and which hotel he's going to stay at.
b Listen to the second one and say what kind of room he wants, and how long he's going to stay at the hotel.

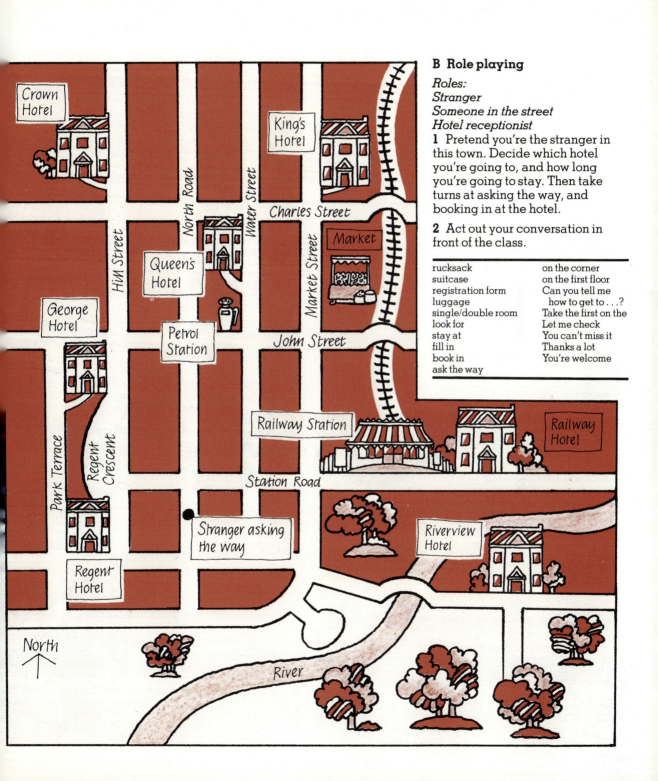

B Role playing

Roles:
Stranger
Someone in the street
Hotel receptionist

1 Pretend you're the stranger in this town. Decide which hotel you're going to, and how long you're going to stay. Then take turns at asking the way, and booking in at the hotel.

2 Act out your conversation in front of the class.

rucksack	on the corner
suitcase	on the first floor
registration form	Can you tell me how to get to . . .?
luggage	Take the first on the
single/double room	Let me check
look for	You can't miss it
stay at	Thanks a lot
fill in	You're welcome
book in	
ask the way	

19 What are they going to do about it?

A Open class discussion

1 Study the plan of the town and say why there is a traffic problem.

2 Look at the improvement plan and say what changes they're going to make in this town.

3 On the tape is a conversation between a couple who live in this town. They're discussing one of the proposed by-passes. Say how they feel about it. Then give your own opinion of the improvement plan.

B Group discussion

1 Make a list of the problems in your city, town, or village (traffic, pollution, water, rubbish, unemployment, etc.) Say whether they're doing anything about them, or what they're going to do about them.

1 ....
2 ....
3 ....
4 ....

2 Now make a list of national problems and say what the government is going to do about them.

1 ....
2 ....
3 ....
4 ....

3 Do you have any family or personal problems? If so, say what you're going to do about them.

solution	pass a law
traffic jam	go right through
water shortage	a good idea
taxes	they say they're
poverty	going to
improve	the answer to
extend	narrow/wide
build	dangerous
pull down	

Town Plan

Old building
Park
To West Coast
Town Gate
Town Hall
Castle
To West Coast
To West Coast

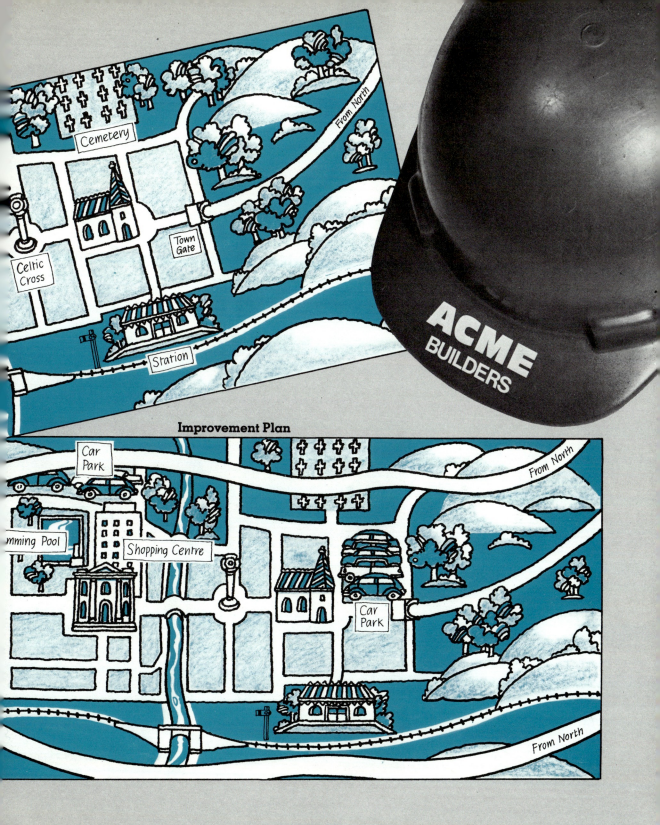

Improvement Plan

20 Are you a dreamer?

Here is an account of a very famous dream. It is the strange dream that Abraham Lincoln had.

'Ten days ago, I dreamed that I heard sobs as if a number of people were quietly weeping. I went from one room to another, but saw no-one. However, the sobbing followed me as I went along. Every object I saw was familiar to me, but I couldn't see the people who were weeping. I was puzzled and worried. When I entered the East Room, I saw a corpse in funeral vestments. There were soldiers around it acting as guards, and there was a crowd of people looking sadly at the corpse. "Who is dead in the White House?" I asked one of the soldiers. "The President", he answered. "He was killed by an assassin." Then I woke up.'

A little after ten o'clock in the evening, on Friday, April 14, 1865—the night he told his friends about this dream—Abraham Lincoln was assassinated.

nice	visions
strange	a coincidence
nasty	a dream come true
unpleasant	I'm sure
worried	I think
symbols	I don't think

SURRAT.   BOOTH.   HAROLD.

War Department, Washington, April 20, 1865,

 # $100,000 REWARD!

THE MURDERER

Of our late beloved President, Abraham Lincoln,

IS STILL AT LARGE.

$50,000 REWARD

Will be paid by this Department for his apprehension, in addition to any reward offered by Municipal Authorities or State Executives.

$25,000 REWARD

Will be paid for the apprehension of JOHN H. SURRATT, one of Booth's Accomplices.

$25,000 REWARD

Will be paid for the apprehension of David C. Harold, another of Booth's accomplices.

LIBERAL REWARDS will be paid for any information that shall conduce to the arrest of either of the above-named criminals, or their accomplices.

All persons harboring or secreting the said persons, or either of them, or aiding or assisting their concealment or escape, will be treated as accomplices in the murder of the President and the attempted assassination of the Secretary of State, and shall be subject to trial before a Military Commission and the punishment of DEATH.

Let the stain of innocent blood be removed from the land by the arrest and punishment of the murderers.

All good citizens are exhorted to aid public justice on this occasion. Every man should consider his own conscience charged with this solemn duty, and rest neither night nor day until it be accomplished.

EDWIN M. STANTON, Secretary of War.

DESCRIPTIONS.—BOOTH is Five Feet 7 or 8 inches high, slender build, high forehead, black hair, black eyes, and wears a heavy black moustache.

JOHN H. SURRAT is about 5 feet, 9 inches. Hair rather thin and dark; eyes rather light; no beard. Would weigh 145 or 150 pounds. Complexion rather pale and clear, with color in his cheeks. Wore light clothes of fine quality. Shoulders square; cheek bones rather prominent; chin narrow; ears projecting at the top; forehead rather low and square, but broad. Parts his hair on the right side; neck rather long. His lips are firmly set. A slim man.

DAVID C. HAROLD is five feet six inches high, hair dark, eyes dark, eyebrows rather heavy, full face, nose short, hand short and fleshy, feet small, instep high, round bodied, naturally quick and active, slightly closes his eyes when looking at a person.

NOTICE.—In addition to the above, State and other authorities have offered rewards amounting to almost one hundred thousand dollars, making an aggregate of about TWO HUNDRED THOUSAND DOLLARS.

A Open class discussion

1 Do you think this dream was just a coincidence? Or did Abraham Lincoln dream it because he was worried? Give your opinion.

2 Tell the class about other famous dreams. Abraham Lincoln's dream was unpleasant. Can you think of any nice dreams?

3 Listen to the tape: then complete the information in the box about the meaning of colours in dreams.

Colours	Meaning
	Affection
	Strong love
	Violent passion
	Domination
	Happiness
	Death
	Strong hate

4 Give your opinions of these colour symbols.

B Small group discussion

1 Tell the group about your dreams:

how often you dream
whether your dreams are nice or nasty
whether you dream in colours
if your dreams ever come true

Ask the group about their dreams.

2 What did you used to dream about when you were a child?

3 What is day-dreaming? Do you ever day-dream? Tell one another about your day-dreams.

Oxford University Press, Walton Street, Oxford OX2 6DP

Oxford London Glasgow New York Toronto Melbourne Wellington
Kuala Lumpur Singapore Hong Kong Tokyo Delhi Bombay
Calcutta Madras Karachi Nairobi Dar Es Salaam Cape Town

ISBN 0 19 432216 5   (Student's book 1)
ISBN 0 19 432217 3   (Student's book 2)
ISBN 0 19 432218 1   (Student's book 3)
ISBN 0 19 432219 X   (Teacher's book)

First published 1980
Second impression 1981

Printed in Spain by Mateu Cromo Artes
Graficas S.A.